One and twenty poems

AF624652

Charlotte Rose Noble

BookLeaf Publishing
India | USA | UK

Presentation by *BookLeaf Publishing*

Web: www.bookleafpub.com

E-mail: info@bookleafpub.com

ISBN: 9789357444873

First edition 2022

DEDICATION

For my family.

You

He was bemused
By his belief,
He was proud and gratified
And internally satisfied.
He had a craving endeavor
To become better.
It was his ambition to pursue,
To find a better version of his 'you.'

Fantasize

My eyes are closed
Yet but open
They see the scene
Of things in dreams.
Hidden of truth and realities.
Seeking escape from all those who are mean
And the world's brutalities.
My thoughts traveling through my bloodstream
Going on an Odyssey.
Electrical compulsions
Is my mind an atrocity?
I am responsible for my own dishonesty.
Lost in my own mythology,
Corruption and my mind's abductions.
Immodesty and curiosity,
Blinded by my fantasies
Disorientated in the ecstasy
I am disconnected in actuality.
Seeking relief in my daydreams
Distorted my belief
Which hides all my grief.
These lies bring no practicality
Only to some degree
Of my mind's falsehoods.
My dreams bring no good

I should rid myself of these fantasies.
I agonize in my abnormalities
And this world's formalities.
I live happily in my delusions,
I have eternal immortality in my false realities.
I am in harmony with my exclusion and
illusions.
In my mind there is no confusion,
I am gratified and satisfied
In all that I fantasize.

The Sweet Thought of Love

Love is but a flower,
Blossoms with tenderness and care.
Grows as time passes,
And strengthen with each sunlight's day.
A tiny break, it can be repaired.
But with many it will wither.

The Princess

She was envious of the birds flight,
Which soars through the sky's height.
Day by day went wasting away,
Never would she disobey.
There she stayed, there she sat
But inside she was a wildcat.
She desired to be like the bird.
Though she was silent and never heard.
All her cries were internally
And presented normality externally.

She dreamt and longed
For a place where she truly belongs.
She was sweet and innocent and only sixteen
But her mind was wild and full of dreams.
The Princess secretly wished she would be exiled
But upon her face was a false smile.
Maybe she was selfish,
Maybe she was foolish.
To her, her world was cruel, with people who relish
Of her fame and where jealous.
She was only in pain,
And at the mercy of those who reign.

The Princess had to abstain from many joys.
She had no voice, no choice, only used in their ploys.

She had no gambit of her escape
And made no mistakes.
There was an internal debate
To stay and live in misery
Or leave to a life of mystery.
She pounded upon the thought
Maybe she could be free like the hawk
And flee before her jubilee.
The Princess would become an escapee
With no guarantee of her safety.

Sixteen came and left.
She was now more depressed.
And maybe a little insane.
The Princess could no longer be contained.
She wished to be free
And live carefree.
The Princess planned
To leave her homeland.
She was scared, she was afraid
She had to persuade her mind not to be delayed.
Now she believed it was her fate,
To escape through the gate
And the towering fence.
The Princess must commence,

Her escape,
Before they awake.
The Princess had to be discreet
So she could make her fleet.
Her internal battle did not subside,
Inside her heart, it still cried.
She questioned must she really leave
For a world she did not know but only grieved.
"Would this unknown world be glorious?
Or would it be notorious?"

The Princess had made up her mind.
It was now the time.
She had to evade
All those she used to obey.

So one quiet night,
She took her flight.
When all those were asleep
She began to creep.
She left the palace, her prison
For a new place, where she must be hidden.
The Princess wore a disguise,
And took a bag of supplies.
And creeped away in the night.
The hallway was lit by candlelight.
She climbed the gate
And made her escape.
The Princess was free at last.

She left her name in the past.

The night's air was cold.
She took a hold of her cloak in which it had a pocket of gold.
And ventured further into her adventure.
The Princess would never surrender.
She waited for first morning light,
The Princess hardly slept that cold night.
When the people awoke
She hid within her cloak.
The Princess, she was no more.
She had no escorts and would no longer be adored.
She felt like a foreigner,
Now she was nothing but a simple commoner.
She traded some gold and a smokey quartz
For a fair black horse.

She would travel across the land
Through the burning sand.
She would continue to roam
Until she would find her new home.
With the horse as her fellow adventurer
On this dangerous venture.
She traveled far away from the palace, no long bound,
And never to be found.

Sunrise

The dawn will come,
The sun will rise.
Some may stay and lie
Others will awake.
For every day it brings a new.
Though yesterday will never leave.
Dragging our past
Like our own shadow.
With the world alight
Our darkest comes from our own selves.
Mocking us, taunting us
“Quiet!” Internal voice yells,
Desperate to escape the mind.
To find purpose, to find meaning.
With each day we must find our own joy.
To ignite that spark,
To kindle that flame within our heart.
To ignore those self sabotaging thoughts
And draw upon the light.
With each new day
Is a promised sunrise.

The Flower

The flower but white
wished to be green.
To be thought of
And never seen.
Not to be on display,
With people plucking at it, day by day.
To be apart of the leafy green crowd,
Safe and blended,
Not causing a scene.
To be not a prize,
Not worthy of catching eyes.
To be sheltered and hidden.
As to be beautiful can be one’s own demise.
Some cannot help themselves,
From stealing the flower for themselves.

Dream

Dream the leisure
You so deeply desire.
Imagine the hope
Without the constriction of ropes.
Let your mind ponder
For something fonder.
Believe that you can achieve,
That you will receive,
Your finest aspiration.
You will reach your destination.
This infatuation will proceed,
Helping you to succeed.
You feel it in your soul,
That you will reach your goal.

Sky

Could I fly
Upon up to the sky?
High into the night,
To the bright
Stars above.
Where the light and love,
Come shining down
Without a single sound.

My Kin

Green eyes,
That is mine.
Light hair, light skin.
Though my kin,
Have dark skin
And a sparkle in their dark eyes.
They are all truly mine.

Feeble

This without seeds or land they can sow
Will recognised and antagonize
All the things they cannot grow.
It will show in their hollow
Faces with the tint of yellow
In their eyes.
Some will try and hide their demise.
To be common and poor,
Is to be thought of no more.
Prominent ribs hidden under
Layer of rags and covers.
For which they call clothes.
They may wallow in their woes.
Harshness is marked
By the coldness at dark.
The cold chill,
Will make many ill.
The struggle can be fatal
For the feeble
But that morbid end
Will be peaceful.

The Breeze

Hath the wind blows.
Only power some know.
A whimsical breeze
To an icy cold freeze.
Easing hot flushed cheeks and sending kites
To scoring heights.
Pollinating trees
And the halting singing of buzzing bees.
Sometimes the wind can be a salvation.
Or sounding its song in the empty abyss like a damnation.

Creating a cooler breeze along the coast,
The sea's aroma will leave you engrossed.
Mountain and valley breezes can prevail,
To the coastal winds that make boats sail.
Powering the transportation of their voyage
At the mercy of the windage.
Being set off course and blown,
Traveling far away from home.
This ocean journey can lead to shipwreck
Leaving those stranded to flee the deck.

A wrath seeking vengeance,
You will experience the ambience.

Sometimes a sweet breeze
Or a hurricane destroying whole cities.
A power that can overbear
This simple thing is called air.

My Baby

Sweet little cheeks,
Chubby little fingers,
I've only known you a week,
I speak to you in whispers,
My baby, my love,
The nights have been rough
They have been long.
It may be tough,
But you are my sweet song.
You make me laugh
You make me smile.
My little baby.

Happiness

It is all in your head,
Effecting what you heard and said.
Sometimes it's true,
Sometimes it's false.
Real or not, it’s all in your mind.
You decide,
How you feel,
You decide,
To make it real.
Sad or happy, it's up to you
To choose what is true.

Light

Walking in darkness
Will only cause despair.
Desperate to resurface
To breathe fresh air.
Seeking out goodness
To a path of luminousness.
Taking no steps backwards.
Forward,
And continuous.
No matter how tenuous.
Be there, in the light,
Even in the dark of night.

Inner Voice

Sometimes
It takes a little time
To realize
What is right before our eyes.
We blind ourselves
With our minds
With truth covered in falsehood.
We take a stand of what stood,
Before us but not before us.
Confusions we must discuss,
With our inner voice
That makes all that noise.
Yet it is quiet to the seeing eyes.
That inner voice believes to be wise,
But mostly it is full of lies,
That we must learn to recognise.

Volatile

The sadness
Struck her and no one understood,
That it came upon sudden,
Without reason,
Without place.
She swallowed and grieved
Nothing to be seen.
Then it was gone again.
She returned,
Back again.
She was herself.
Happy and free,
Living life normally.

Ticking

The persistent clock,
Never ceases to stop.
Its mockery and taunting,
Is ever so haunting.
'Let me be!'
I plea.
Alas it does not.
It will never stop.
Only I will cease to be.
But the clock will always be,
Ticking.

Not Me

It may be better
In this weather,
But that does not
Mean I ought,
To go.
So you know,
That you can count,
Me out.

Fly

If I jump, will I fly?
I am too scared to try?
To see,
What will happen to me?
What will I be?
Will I die,
Or reach the sky?
To stay forever still
Or soar high with a thrill?
What will I choose?
What will I lose?
Will I ever soar high,
Up in the sky?

Real Me

I believe that sometimes I am wrong,
That I truly do not belong.
I am different, you see.
People do not know the real me.
I put on my face,
For the world to see,
But that is not the real me.
I am somewhere hidden
Within my head,
With actions dreamt of
But never said.
"Would they like the real me?"
That they will never see.

The Absent Plan

Planning would have been best.
Weeks and weeks
Just past by
With nothing
Done.
That night came.
Alongside it came
Time.
It was running.
Planning would have been best.
But now we must live with regrets.

www.ingramcontent.com/pod-product-compliance
Lightning Source LLC
Chambersburg PA
CBHW051758130826
49812CB00033B/1197
* 9 7 8 9 3 5 7 4 4 4 8 7 3 *